P9-DGS-735

STAGE 2

Why Do Leaves Change Color?

BY BETSY MAESTRO
ILLUSTRATED BY LORETTA KRUPINSKI

HarperCollins*Publishers*

The *Let's-Read-and-Find-Out Science* book series was originated by Dr. Franklyn M. Branley, Astronomer Emeritus and former Chairman of the American Museum—Hayden Planetarium, and was formerly co-edited by him and Dr. Roma Gans, Professor Emeritus of Childhood Education, Teachers College, Columbia University. Text and illustrations for each book in the series are checked for accuracy by an expert in the relevant field. For a complete catalog of Let's-Read-and-Find-Out Science books, write to HarperCollins Children's Books, 10 East 53rd Street, New York, NY 10022.

Let's Read-and-Find-Out Science is a registered trademark of HarperCollins Publishers.

Library of Congress Cataloging-in-Publication Data
Maestro, Betsy.
    Why do leaves change color? / by Betsy Maestro ; illustrated by
Loretta Krupinski.
        p.   cm. – (Let's-read-and-find-out science. Stage 2)
    Summary: Explains how leaves change their colors in autumn and then
separate from the tree as the tree prepares for winter.
    ISBN 0-06-022873-3. – ISBN 0-06-022874-1 (lib. bdg.)
    ISBN 0-06-445126-7 (pbk.)
    1. Leaves–Color–Juvenile literature.   2. Fall foliage–Juvenile literature.
[1. Leaves.   2. Fall foliage.]   I. Krupinski, Loretta, ill.   II. Title.
III. Series.
QK649.M27   1994   93-9611
582.16'0497–dc20   CIP
                                                                        AC

1 2 3 4 5 6 7 8 9 10 ❖
First Edition

The illustrations in this book were done with gouache and color pencil on
Strathmore 500 Bristol board paper.

Why Do Leaves Change Color?

Look at the leaves! It's autumn, and leaves are turning red and yellow, gold and brown.

Each type of tree has its own kind of leaves. The colors of autumn leaves differ from tree to tree. Some oak leaves may be brown or yellow, while maple leaves may turn bright red.

Leaves come in different sizes and shapes as well as colors. Some leaves are wide, and others narrow. Some have points, while others may be rounded. How many different kinds can you find?

Sugar Maple

Red Maple

Tulip

White Oak

Sassafras

Black Birch

Silver Maple

Norway Maple

Gray Birch

Red Oak

7

8

Just a few weeks ago, all the leaves were green. Back in the spring, the tiny new leaves uncurled from their buds.

The green color in the leaves helps them to absorb or hold sunlight. Chlorophyll gives the leaves their green coloring. Chlorophyll is a natural coloring called a pigment.

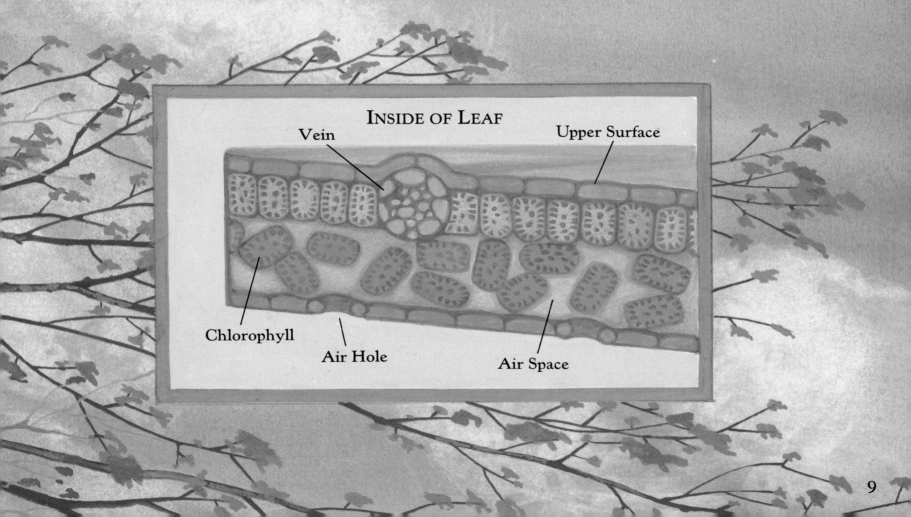

INSIDE OF LEAF

Vein

Upper Surface

Chlorophyll

Air Hole

Air Space

Leaves are very important to the tree. They make a kind of sugar that is the tree's food. Leaves need sunlight, water, and air to make this food.

The leaves work to feed the tree all summer long. The sugar is used by all parts of the tree–the leaves, branches, trunk, and roots. The food, or sugar, helps the tree to grow. Extra sugar is stored in the leaves.

In the fall, many things are changing. In many places, there is a change in the weather. There are changes in light and temperature. Inside the leaves, there will be many changes too. All of these changes bring about the beautiful colors of fall.

In the fall, there are fewer hours of sunlight each day. The change in light tells the tree to get ready for winter. Winter is a time of rest for the tree. When winter comes, the tree will have to survive with less water and sunlight.

14

The tree begins to get ready for its winter rest. It needs very little food now, and the leaves stop their work. The life of the leaves is almost at an end. The tree no longer needs them.

When the leaves die, they will fall from the tree. This will happen slowly over a number of weeks. As the leaves begin to separate from the tree, they get less water. Without water, the leaves cannot make new chlorophyll. The old chlorophyll begins to fade. The green color starts to disappear.

Now, other colors can be seen in the leaves. Other pigments have been in the leaves all along. But they were hidden by the dark green of the chlorophyll. Once the green color fades, the yellow and orange pigments can be seen.

These pigments give color to the leaves of birches, poplars, and elms. Some foods like bananas and carrots get their natural yellow and orange coloring from these same pigments. They also give color to some flowers. Maybe you can think of some.

Aspen (Poplar)

Elm

Gray Birch

White Birch

Sugar Maple

Red Maple

White Oak

Elm

18

Autumn leaves have other colors as well. The yellows and oranges have been in the leaves all along. Other pigments are made as the leaves begin to die. These new pigments are made from the extra sugar stored in the leaves.

Sunlight causes the stored sugar to change to pigment. The new pigments make some leaves turn red, rust, or purple. The more sugar there is, the brighter the colors will be. Bright days and cool nights seem to bring out the best fall colors.

Red Oak

Gray Birch

Maple leaves get their red color from these new pigments. Many flowers, and some foods such as beets and radishes, get their color from these red pigments. The brilliant red of sumac leaves shows up only in the fall, when these pigments form.

Some trees, like oaks, make tannin in the fall. Tannin is not a pigment, but it does color the leaves. Some oak leaves turn a rich brown color in autumn. See if you can find some. You may still be able to see some green coloring too.

Red Maple

White Oak

Sumac

Red Oak

21

The changing color of autumn leaves is caused by changes in weather and light. This is why the colors are not the same every year. The best leaf colors usually come with lots of bright sunshine and crisp, clear nights. Too much rain may make the colors dull. An early frost may kill the leaves too soon.

Evergreen trees, like pines and spruces, keep their leaves all year. But in cool climates, other trees must lose their leaves to survive in winter.

After the leaves have changed color, they are ready to separate from the tree. When they are just barely hanging on, a little bit of wind or rain will make them fall to the ground.

In just a short time, the tree will begin to look bare. Piles of dead leaves collect under the tree. Some will blow away. Others will be raked up. The leaves that are left will begin to rot. Over time, they will become part of the soil. Rotting leaves enrich the soil with minerals the tree needs to stay healthy.

When the last of the leaves have fallen, the tree is ready for winter. During the cold weather, the tree will be dormant, or resting. New leaf buds have already formed. Next spring, they will open and begin to make food for the tree.

But now, in fall, it's time to enjoy the colors of the leaves. Beautiful

autumn foliage cannot be seen everywhere. Only some places, such as New England, have displays of many colors. This is because the weather conditions there are usually just right and there are so many different kinds of trees.

Fall is a time to have fun with leaves. It's a time to take in the sights and sounds of the leaves. It's a time for jumping into great piles of leaves—and then sometimes, a time for raking them up. Fall is a time to get ready for winter. The trees are ready—are you?

Here are some things you can do with leaves:

Make a Leaf Rubbing

1) Collect some different kinds of leaves. You will need leaves that are not dry or crumbly.
2) Arrange up to 4 leaves on a smooth surface.
3) Put a thin sheet of white paper over your leaves.
4) Remove the paper from around a dark-colored crayon.
5) Use the side of the crayon to rub gently over your paper and leaves.
6) Watch the outlines and vein lines of your leaves appear on your paper.

Press Some Leaves

You can keep the most beautiful leaves you find by pressing them with an iron.

1) Put an old cloth or towel on an ironing board or table.

2) Arrange your leaves between two sheets of waxed paper on the covered ironing board.

3) Have a grown-up help you to preheat an iron. It does not have to be very hot.

5) Iron the waxed paper. The iron will seal and press your leaves. They will look very nice and will last for a long time.

Do not use a hot iron by yourself. You must ask a grown-up to help you.

Colorful fall foliage can be seen all across the United States during the months of September and October. Plan a trip with your family to see the colors. Here are some suggestions for places to visit:

- **Green Mountain National Forest**: 151 West Street, P.O. Box 519, Rutland, VT 05701 (802) 747–6700

  Take a drive along State Route 100, which borders the forest, from Killington north to Waterbury.

- **Mark Twain National Forest**: 401 Fairgrounds Road, Rolla, MO 65401 (314) 364–4621

  Visit the Fall Color Festival (call (417) 683–4594) or take the Glade Top Trail from Ava to Fairview.

- **Superior National Forest**: 515 W. First Street, P.O. Box 338, Duluth, MN 55801 (218) 720–5324

  Take the self-guided Sawtooth Mountain Fall Color Tour: the Sawtooth Mountain Range parallels Lake Superior's shoreline from East Beaver Bay to the Cascade River.

- **Willamette National Forest**: 211 E. Seventh Avenue, P.O. Box 10607, Eugene, OR 97440 (503) 465–6521

  Travel the McKenzie Pass/Santiam Pass Loop: From Eugene take Highway 126 east to Highway 242 and the Old McKenzie Highway, continue to Sisters and then head west on Highway 20 back over the Santiam Pass.

- **Rio Grande National Forest**: 1803 West U.S. Highway 160, Monte Vista, CO 81144 (719) 852–5941

  Take a drive along the Silver Thread Scenic Byway, Colorado Highway 149, from South Fork to Lake City.

- **Chattanooga, TN**: *Annual Fall Color Cruise and Folk Festival in late October at Tennessee River Nickajack Reservation; Exit 158 off of Interstate 24: 25 miles southwest of downtown Chattanooga. Call 1–800–766–2784.*

- **Blue Ridge Parkway**: National Park Service, 220 BB&T Building, Asheville, NC 28801 (704) 298–0398

  Take a drive on the parkway, which extends from Cherokee, North Carolina, at the edge of the Great Smoky Mountains, to the Shenandoah Valley in Virginia.

For information about foliage which is updated weekly, call the national "Fall Color Hotline" sponsored by the U.S. Forest Service: 1–800–354–4595.